A Dialogue of Suffering

Between the Crucifixion and the Holocaust

By Rick Wienecke

Copyright © 2015 Rick Wienecke

All rights reserved, except where noted.

Scripture quotations are from THE HOLY BIBLE: NEW INTERNATIONAL VERSION®. NIV®. Copyright © 1973, 1978, 1984 by Biblica. All rights reserved worldwide.

Scripture quotations marked NLT are taken from the Holy Bible, New Living Translation, copyright 1996. Used by permission of Tyndale House Publishers, Inc., Wheaton, Illinois 60189. All rights reserved.

Contributors to this curriculum:

Pam Jarvis, Geoff Barnard and Mike Jarvis

Photos: © 2011 Mike Jarvis & © 2014 Petra van der Zande

ISBN 978-965-7542-29-3

This book can be ordered by contacting:

- www.castingseeds.com
- castingseeds@gmail.com
- tsurtsinapublications@gmail.com
- www.lulu.com

A Tsur Tsina Production

Printed by PRINTIV, Jerusalem, Israel

TABLE OF CONTENTS

Introduction	5
Why Have a Dialogue of Suffering?	6
Directions	7
Gethsemane - Suffering and Death	9
Panel # 1 – "Father, forgive them, for they know not what they do."	12
Panel # 2 – "Today you will be with me in paradise."	20
Panel # 3 – "Mother this is your son, son this is your mother."	28
Panel # 4 – "My God my God, why have you forsaken me?"	36
Panel # 5 – "I am thirsty."	46
Panel # 6 – "It is finished."	52
Panel # 7 – "Into your hands I commit my spirit."	58
Epilogue - The Butterfly - Healing and Life	66
The Final Embrace and the Empty Cup	69
About Rick Wienecke	72
Preview of Rick's Biography "Seeds in the Wind"	73

Introduction

How did it come about?

Where does a prayer begin?

Does it happen at the same time the tear starts to fall, or has it always been there, waiting for the right moment to express itself?

I call it a suddenly . . . when the timing of God and His will intersect.

God started to show me something in 2001 with a number of emotional interactions I know could only have been initiated by Him. Collectively, they became the "suddenlies" drawing my attention to a question: "Could the Holocaust and the Crucifixion have something in common? Could an understanding exist between these two personalities through their common sufferings?" Church history had always separated these two, but could there be a "Dialogue of Suffering" through art that might join the two?

The idea profoundly scared me. The places and personalities of the Holocaust and the Crucifixion appeared unapproachable. For almost a full year, I argued with God about my participation in the idea.

My final argument was, "How could I create a memorial to the six million who perished in the Holocaust if I don't have memory of it myself?" I am not Jewish, so I don't have within my own family a resource of memory to draw from. I am Canadian born, not European, so I don't even have a geographical memory to create from. I thought this was a good argument and convinced myself for a time it was not for me to do.

Suddenly I felt the Lord say to me, "But I do . . . I have a memory of every man, every woman, every child, every train car, every camp, every pit, every cry from every gas chamber. . . . I have a memory of it all. You can create from my memory, not yours."

And so the prayer began….

Why Have a Dialogue of Suffering?

A person who wants to be understood in his sufferings knows that he is about to make himself vulnerable. He must take the chance to speak, with a hope that the other party will hear and understand, and somehow begin to identify with his pain. Therein lies the possibility for that pain and suffering to finally be heard and a useful dialogue to begin.

This curriculum is an opportunity for you to take a good look at the personalities of the Holocaust and the Crucifixion. It is also an examination of the seven words spoken from the Crucifixion and the often unspoken words from the Holocaust. To look at the visual nature of the art work itself. To ultimately ask the questions, "How is the Father's heart involved in these two? Why does He attach His tears and memory so strongly to *both* of these sons?"

The Curriculum is *not in any way* an intellectual exercise to somehow frame and bring an understanding into the place of suffering between these two personalities. You *must* be willing to live in the tension of not knowing the answers, and to allow God the Father to share His tears one layer at a time, *in the questions...*

We may never fully understand.

Directions

The curriculum is designed to be covered in a series of 1½-2 hour meetings, ideally one section per week.

Assemble these tools before you begin:

1. The *Bible*, in book form or online. Unless otherwise noted, the *New International Version (NIV)* of the *Bible* has been used as the reference text for the entire curriculum. *Biblos* on the web (http://biblos.com) is a great free online resource with numerous translations and study tools.
2. The Fountain of Tears DVD.
3. The *Dialogue of Suffering* workbook (this publication).

After you have assembled the tools above:

a. Your first meeting should begin by viewing the entire *Fountain of Tears* DVD, followed by a time of discussion about your overall impressions of the *Fountain of Tears*, its meanings, and its implications.
b. Begin subsequent meetings by (again) watching the portion of *Fountain of Tears* video that coincides with the panel you are studying.
c. Read the objectives and commentary in your workbook.
d. Complete the discussion questions.
e. Optional: complete any additional study notes and activities.

Gethsemane - Suffering and Death

There is so much attached to this word "Gethsemane": it is a place of darkness and horror and of an intense struggle of wills. But it is also a garden where olives are harvested and crushed to bring out oil, used in Bible times for healing and for anointing of kings. In this darkest of all nights, the will to live was crushed and pressed in order to give the oil of life, because Somebody asked Him to do so, not simply by dying, which might have eased the struggle, but by way of a slow, methodically crafted torture, a death designed to inflict the maximum amount of pain for the longest possible time.

In a small way the Gethsemane sculpture reflected how I felt before creating the "Fountain of Tears". It was such a struggle to start this God-ordained commission. I knew it would cost me everything and that I might lose all my friends. It had been a miracle that I, the Gentile, had received Israeli citizenship – a sign from heaven I was to stay in Israel, to become a part, to learn the language. I had joined the kibbutz and served in the IDF. God had given me a love for these people, and the relationships that had been forged reflected God's hand on it all. It was such an honor to be part of this people. Was there a possibility I could lose it all?

The Holocaust is one of the deepest threads running through the fabric of this country. Touching this subject almost felt like entering something so holy that it was better avoided. It was a place one approached with questions, but never with answers. How could I connect the terrible memories of the Holocaust to Jesus' crucifixion and His last seven words?
My Israeli friends would be infuriated that I, the Gentile claiming to be their friend, dared to create a dialogue between those two events that only cursed each other.

"Can there be a dialogue reflecting each other's pain?" I wondered. "Can there be a fellowship of suffering between the two that will bring a cleansing and healing to all this misunderstanding and deep hatred?"
The struggle with this commission was like a personal Gethsemane to me; my own justifications and those self-preserving arguments had to die; now I had to begin sculpting.

"Oh Lord that my head was a spring of water and my eyes a fountain of tears, that I would weep day and night for the lost of my people." Jeremiah 9

Knowing that this journey was not just the sculpting of a large project but a journey of prayer and intercession, I wondered where to start.
Gethsemane, perhaps? In a sense, that was where the crucifixion began.
In this place, the Father showed the Son what lay in front of Him.
The Holocaust - could this garden scene resemble all those nights in which the Jewish people were rounded up and sent to prisons or camps?

For Jesus it was the night of His captivity, when they bound him and led Him away. Different steps had been taken between the time of His imprisonment and His final judgment. After a lot of political maneuvering and manipulations came the final solution - His death by crucifixion. The Jewish people were first bound by the Nuremberg Laws and then led into captivity to the ghettos until the SS put the final solution into action, death in the gas chambers , crucifixion.

I sculpted the Jesus figure as being poured out over a large stone, as if His body took on the very shape of the stone. The focus of His struggle is represented in the cup of suffering which He holds, allegorically pictured in the shape of a cup that is filled to the brim with suffering. As the Father showed the Son everything that was in the cup, His sweat mixed with drops of blood flowed over the stone. Would He even have known that there would be a moment of total abandonment by the Father? And then the Father asked His Son to drink of this horror for the sake of salvation for those who had been the very ones to persecute and hate Him.

In the sculpture Jesus holds the cup in His left hand, fully extending His arm, as far away from His mouth as possible. The cup is balanced between His index finger and thumb, while the other three fingers are free from holding it. This symbolizes Jesus' indecision, the three fingers representing the three times He called to His disciples to pray with Him but found them asleep. Three times He prayed to the Father that the cup would be removed from Him. In that darkest of all nights He alone made the terrible decision, "Father, if it is Your will, take this cup from me, nevertheless not my will, but Your will be done."

The crucifixion began the moment Jesus agreed to drink the cup of suffering.

"Father, forgive them, for they do not know what they are doing."

Panel 1

First word of the seven last words from the crucifixion

> *Jesus said, "Father, forgive them, for they do not know what they are doing." And they divided up his clothes by casting lots.*
>
> Luke 23:34

Key word: *Forgiveness*

Objectives

In this section you will learn:

1. To define the word "covenant."
2. To understand the concept of *"forgiveness."*
3. To discover the idea of a "Covenant of *Forgiveness.*"
4. To explore the Holocaust survivor's reasoning for *forgiveness* leading to forgetting.
5. To analyze how we, as followers of Jesus, can embrace the crucifixion as our covenant of *forgiveness*, then turn and blame the Jews for His death?

Artist's Introduction: Rick Wienecke

When I stand in front of the fountain, I stand as an Israeli, a believer in Jesus, and an artist. However, my main and central identity is a believer in Jesus; all other self-descriptions were birthed out of this. So I thought to myself, *Out of the seven last utterances Jesus spoke from the crucifixion, which was the first? Besides the Lord Himself, does anyone really know the exact order?* But my thinking led me also to ask, *What would be the most important to Jesus? If these are His last moments of life, what would be the first thing that comes to His mind?* Perhaps it is, "Father, *forgive* them for they know not what they do."

Background

In Panel #1, *forgiveness* is the key. Jesus is pleading with the Father for those who are killing Him. He is trying to reason with the Father that they didn't know what they were doing when they delivered Him to the Romans, or when the Romans nailed Him to the cross.

Forgiveness and Covenant

At the crucifixion, Jesus is not only *forgiving* those who crucified Him, but He is also creating in those words, "Father *forgive* them they know not what they do," a covenant based on *forgiveness*, which becomes the New Covenant.
Therefore, in keeping with the definition of covenant, if I receive *forgiveness*, I must also *forgive*. This is what Jesus is demonstrating in the covenant of *forgiveness* on the cross. It is the very heart and character of His sacrifice: *forgiveness*.

The Holocaust Survivor's Dilemma

In receiving *forgiveness* I have to give *forgiveness* out. This is the beginning of the dilemma for the Holocaust survivor. The Holocaust survivor will attach the word *"forgiveness"* to the word "forget," and he cannot forget the perished of his people. In the forgetting comes the dilemma of *forgiveness* for the survivor. Does the Holocaust survivor have a wrong concept of the word *"forgiveness"*? Has he embraced a lie?

The Holocaust Survivor's Reasoning: Forgiveness Leads to Forgetting

In trying to understand the mind-set of a Jewish Holocaust survivor, let's read what a survivor of the Auschwitz concentration camp, Ellie Wiesel, says in his book, Night: "For the survivor who chooses to testify, it is clear: his duty is to bear witness for the dead and for the living. He has no right to deprive future generations of a past that belongs to our collective memory. To forget would not only be dangerous but offensive; to forget the dead would be akin to killing them a second time . . . . The witness has forced himself to testify, for the youth of today, for the children who will be born tomorrow. He does not want his past to become their future."[1]
Is it that the survivor of such a horrific act fears these inhuman acts could be repeated on his future generations if we forget the past? Does he/she believe the pain and memories are so deep they cannot be healed?
Ellie Wiesel also states: "Never shall I forget those moments that murdered my God and my soul and turned my dreams to ashes. Never shall I forget those things, even were I condemned to live as long as God Himself. Never."[2]

---

[1] Elie Wiesel, Night, (USA: Hill & Wang, 1960), Introduction xv.
[2] Wiesel, Night, 32

Forgiveness and Replacement

It is amazing to me that the church who claims Jesus as Lord can aggressively ignore His prayer of *forgiveness* for those who crucified Him. The church has historically branded the Jews as the Christ killers. There is a huge amount of documentation that the church drove the persecution against the Jews. It is almost like Jesus never said the first phrase of the seven. Why do they so ignore this word *"forgiveness"*? Could it mean that when you come against the Jewish people it really shows just how little you know Jesus? Replacement theology doesn't only replace Israel with the church, but it has to replace Jesus for something else. For the church to claim anyone killed Christ negates Gethsemane. Jesus chose the Crucifixion; He says He was born for this purpose: "The Lord has laid on him the iniquity of us all" (Isa. 53:6).

He deliberately became the ultimate sacrifice, the Passover lamb. He was walking out the prophetic picture of the priestly sacrifice. He becomes a priest to all mankind, as His Jewish brothers are the priests of the nations (Gen. 12:2–3). He makes it clear to His disciples that He is going up to Jerusalem to be handed over to the Gentiles to be killed and buried then resurrected. He is deliberate with His plan: Luke 18:31–33 says, "Jesus took the Twelve aside and told them, 'We are going up to Jerusalem, and everything that is written by the prophets about the Son of Man will be fulfilled. He will be handed over to Gentiles. They will mock him, insult him, spit on him, flog him, and kill him. On the third day he will rise again.'"

Jesus says in His prayer for *forgiveness* from the cross that His murderers did not know what they were doing. In the same fashion Joseph in Genesis said to his brothers, "You meant it for evil, but God meant it for good." Both sets of people had evil in their hearts, but at the end of the day, God's plan was fulfilled. God's will is bigger than all of man's determined evil.

Jesus' Godliness through the Crucifixion

If we say Jesus was killed as the result of the will of men, it puts Jesus solely into man's realm and not God incarnate. Jesus as the Son of God had the power and the ability to call upon legions of angels to save Him, but He chose not to escape. He even goes as far as interceding for *forgiveness* for His own killers. In this act, He shows His godliness. His prayer for *forgiveness* creates an on-going relationship with his Jewish brothers and with all men through the New Covenant.

In blaming the Jews for his death, people are in effect negating His act of redemption for sin. This lie also negates the prayer in Gethsemane by ignoring that it was the will of the Father that He die, and the Father did not change His will even when Jesus asked for the cup to pass from Him.

Our Action

Our role is to pour out love and honor on the Jewish people and not to condemn them. We have had *forgiveness* lavished on us for the past 2,000 years. As believers, we are supposed to make the Jews jealous, not afraid and suspicious of us.

In the King James Version, Romans 11:11 states, "I say then, Have they stumbled that they should fall? God forbid: but rather through their fall salvation is come unto the Gentiles, for to provoke them to jealousy."

Summary

How can we as followers of Jesus embrace the Crucifixion as our covenant of *forgiveness*, then turn and blame the Jews for His death? This line of thinking would logically have to lead to Jesus never saying, "Father, *forgive* them!"

Discussion Questions

1. Define the concept of *forgiveness*. How does the covenant of *forgiveness* impact your view about who killed Christ?
2. Have you believed the lie that the Jews killed Jesus? If you have, discuss why. Have your views changed after reading this section? Why or why not?
3. Does the Holocaust survivor have a wrong concept of the word *forgiveness*? Try to empathize with Ellie Wiesel's words in this section. Put yourself in the place of the Holocaust victim in the sculpture in Panel #1. What are you saying as you rest your head against the pillar that represents your loved ones killed in the Holocaust?
4. How does the Holocaust victim *forgive* what was done to him and his loved ones? How does he honor his people *and forgive* the perpetrators?
5. Examine your core value about the Jewish people and the crucifixion of Jesus. Do you have any places in your heart where you have withheld *forgiveness* for the Jews because of the lie that they killed Jesus? Take time to reflect on your heart and hear what the Father has to say to you in prayer about your Jewish brothers and sisters.
6. Discuss Romans 11:11. What is your interpretation? What is your action plan to: "Make Israel jealous?"

"Today you will be with me in paradise."

Panel 2

Second word of the seven last words of Christ

> *Jesus answered him, "I tell you the truth, today you will be with me in paradise."*
>
> Luke 23:43

Key word: *Remembrance*

Objectives

In this section you will learn:

1. To establish the concept of *remembrance* from the heart of the Father and the heart of the thief.
2. To examine the questions "Did the Father hear or *remember* the cries of the Holocaust?" and "Has He forgotten His people?"
3. To explore crucifixion and its significance to the Holocaust.
4. To evaluate our view about salvation as related to the thief on the cross.
5. To identify and demonstrate the concept of *remembrance* in God's holidays.

A Plea for Remembrance

This word I have loved forever! It destroys all the doctrines we have created in order to allow a man to enter salvation. The thief Jesus speaks these words to was presumably never baptized, sprinkled, or submerged, nor did he speak in tongues. All of these rituals may seem significant, but they will always be secondary when touching salvation.

What is the thief asking? He is asking to be *remembered*: "Lord, when You come into Your kingdom please *remember* me." This is an incredible request in the last moments of both the thief's and Jesus' lives, "Please, don't forget me!"

Remembrance

Significant portions of the Bible are dedicated to, even demanding, that we *remember*. As an example, all of God's holidays are dedicated to *remembering*.

Each holiday is connected to a time of *remembrance* in the history of the Jews or their land. Passover is the *remembrance* of the coming out of Egypt. Deuteronomy 5:15 says, "*Remember* that you were slaves in Egypt and that the Lord your God brought you out of there with a mighty hand and an outstretched arm. Therefore the Lord your God has commanded you to observe the Sabbath day."

Purim is the story of Esther, still celebrated today as commanded in Esther 9:28, "These days should be *remembered* and observed in every generation by every family, and in every province and in every city. And these days of Purim should never cease to be celebrated by the Jews, nor should the memory of them die out among their descendants."

Shavuot includes *remembering* the story of Ruth. On this festival day, the entire book of Ruth is read. And Hanukah commemorates the rededication of the Holy Temple at the time of the Maccabean Revolt of the second century BCE.

Even the modern holidays of the state of Israel are built on *remembrance*. Holocaust *Remembrance* Day marks the anniversary of the Warsaw Ghetto uprising. Israel's Independence Day commemorates their declaration of independence in 1948.

Would God Himself forget? The only thing He promises to forget is our sin! To impose judgment as King, He turns His back, but He can only turn for a moment because He is also Father and His heart is always pulled back to His people.

Two Reflections of the Heart of God: King and Father

(Refer to the Panel #2 picture) Both elements of Father and King are shown within this piece. The left hand of the crucifixion is turned down, turned away. This is not a show of judgment but disappointment. The thief to his left is cursing and mocking Him, not wanting to be *remembered*. The thief has forgotten himself, forgetting he is a man in need of God. He has replaced God with himself.

In Panel #2, I have demonstrated the heart of the Father beating within the chest of Jesus. Jesus has physically pulled toward the thief who has in some part recognized who He is. His body is nailed down, but at the same time He is pulling against all resistance to touch the stones and tears that give *remembrance* of death with His words of life.

This piece reflects the heart of Jesus, which is the heart of the Father. The word "Father" is a position of authority carrying great expectations. A father is expected to provide- care for his children, to be a source of wisdom and a place where, within each of his children, they will be welcomed.

The King is the creator of law, thus He must also bring judgment. Judgment can be severe, but it also brings order and peace. The King is bound to enforce His own law, but as He enforces His law He does so with tears as the Father, always wishing His child would turn, repent, and come back into a right relationship with Him. He must at times turn from His child but always with the hope the child will feel the loss of covering and return to Him.

The thought of *remembrance* should give us hope: If Jesus, God incarnate, could respond to the cries of a thief in his last minutes of life, how much more would He *remember* and respond to His own people? "The Israelites groaned in their slavery . . . . God heard their groaning and he remembered his covenant" (Ex.2:23–24). He cannot forget them. They are *His* people! He would *have* to respond to these cries. Six million cries, groans, and tears. . . . If he didn't respond, He would be denying His central role as Father.

Crucifixion

Crucifixion was a torture created to inflict the maximum amount of suffering on the victim for the longest amount of time. It is recorded that some victims of crucifixion hung on the cross for five days. Crucifixion was often performed to terrorize and dissuade the onlookers from perpetrating the crimes punishable by it. Victims were left on display after death so others who attempt dissent might be forewarned. Crucifixion was usually intended to provide a death particularly slow, painful, gruesome, humiliating, and public, using whatever means were most expedient for that goal.

Crucifixion identifies with the tortures of the Holocaust. While a crucifixion was an execution, it was also a humiliation by making the condemned as vulnerable as possible. Although artists have depicted the figure on a cross with a loincloth, it is likely victims were crucified completely naked. This was also the experience of many of the millions who perished in the Holocaust, and this aspect is alluded to in Psalm 22:17–18, "I can count all my bones; people stare and gloat over me. They divide my garments among them and cast lots for my clothing."

As I write this, I can see, in my mind's eye, the emaciated bodies of the living dead in the liberated camps such as Bergen Belsen. After arriving at the death camps, prisoners were forced to give up their belongings. All personal items, including clothes, were removed, divided, and redistributed within the Third Reich. These verses were also fulfilled in the Crucifixion of Jesus: "And they crucified him. Dividing up his clothes, they cast lots to see what each would get" (Mark 15:24).

The Gospel of John is much more explicit: "When the soldiers crucified Jesus, they took his clothes, dividing them into four shares, one for each of them, with the undergarment remaining. This garment was seamless, woven in one piece from top to bottom. 'Let's not tear it,' they said to one another. 'Let's decide by lot who will get it.' This happened that the scripture might be fulfilled which said, 'They divided my garments among them and cast lots for my clothing.' So this is what the soldiers did" (John 19:23–24).

Auschwitz was the primary example of Crucifixion. Auschwitz was divided into two main camps: Auschwitz One and Auschwitz Two, also known as Birkenau. If you were saved from immediate death by being sent to Auschwitz One, you then would go through a slow death through starvation and overwork.

When you were no longer of worth to work, you would be sent to Birkenau and gassed. This was the final part of the execution, a twenty-minute suffocation within the gas chambers. In the first ten minutes, as recorded by witnesses, the cries and the prayers could be heard from within the chambers. During the last ten minutes, the gas silenced all sounds.

These ten minutes of cries were heard millions of times over. The estimated number was more than 2.5 million men, women, and children who died by this slow and painful process. The only heart that has capacity to *remember* all the cries, screams, and prayers of the gas chambers belongs to God Himself. This audible intercession on earth demanded a response from the heart of the Father in heaven.

The Holocaust Survivor's Perspective

In telling the story of the two thieves to a Holocaust survivor, it was explained to her that all three crucified men were speaking out in their last minutes of life. The thief on the left was cursing Jesus, and the thief on the right was begging to be *remembered*.

The Holocaust survivor then said, "I can identify with both of the thieves. We always lived with death immediately before us. On any given day in Auschwitz we, as prisoners, with whatever strength was left to us, would curse and mock God. On another day, we would cry out and ask Him to *remember* us."

From the perspective of a survivor, the hands of the figure reflecting the Holocaust are going in opposite directions. The one hand reaches upward, indentifying with the hand giving life. The second hand goes the other way, recognizing the mocking and the cursing.

Summary

As the artist, I have asked myself, would God reject His people? Would He, their Father, replace them when Jesus demonstrates His desire to save in such an extreme way?

The answer is: God will not and cannot reject His people. He is a loving Father. In the last minutes of His own Son's life, the heart of His Father reached out and gave life to the thief, through His Son. This loving act should reassure all of us the Father *remembers* His people forever.

Discussion Questions

1. What is your concept of *remembrance*?
2. Examine your view of the thief going to paradise with Jesus? How does that match your view or challenge your belief of salvation through Jesus?
3. Why do you think the Jews are commanded to *remember* their history through their holidays?
4. How has God the Father provided for, cared for, and welcomed His people?
5. Read Ezekiel 37:1–12 and then reexamine these verses as they relate to the Holocaust. How is the Father demonstrating His heart to His people?
6. Take a minute and look at the picture of Panel #2. How would you communicate the Father's heart to the Holocaust survivor viewing the crucifixion? Does the pain in the survivor reflect or identify with the crucifixion?
7. How can you *remember* the Jews?
8. Take a minute of meditation to clear your mind, soul, and spirit. Imagine you are viewing a scene from the Holocaust at Auschwitz. How would you pray? What would you tell the Holocaust victim going through this unspeakable horror? What do you think the Father felt and *remembered* during those years?

"He said to his mother,…'here is your son' and to the disciple, 'Here is your mother.'"

Panel 3

Third word of the seven last words of Christ

> *When Jesus saw his mother there, and the disciple whom he loved standing nearby, he said to his mother, "Dear woman, here is your son," and to the disciple, "Here is your mother." From that time on, this disciple took her into his home.*
> *John 19:26–27*

Key word: *Relationship*

Objectives

In this section you will learn:

1. To establish the concept of *relationship* from the new and unnatural bond formed between Mary, the mother of Jesus, and John the beloved.
2. To examine the concept of an unnatural *relationship*.
3. To compare and contrast Isaiah 49:15 in context of the Father's *relational* commitment to Israel.
4. To analyze why the Father created a new and unnatural *relationship* with Jesus.
5. To explore the emotional weight of *relationship* as the Holocaust survivor carries his murdered family, friends, and former lifestyle.

A New Relationship

This word is easy to understand from the point of view of the Crucifixion. This is so reflective of the heart of Jesus. At the height of His own suffering, He is caring for His mother. My thinking in creating the Crucifixion Panel #3 was that He is laying her on the shoulders of a friend, someone He can trust—John, the beloved, the only one of His disciples to stay with Him through all the suffering.

Relationship

The prominent word in Panel #3 is *relationship*. The two words foundational for *relationship* are "trust" and "commitment." Jesus is entrusting and committing His mother into John's care. John must now bear her as his own. Jesus is even giving John His own role of son.

A Mother–Son Relationship

Within nature there can't be a deeper place of memory created then between a mother and a son. The words "Mother, this is your son; son, this is your mother" go beyond the natural; they create a *relationship* out of an unnatural place of suffering . John was not Mary's son, and she was not his mother; but the words from the Crucifixion create the closest of all *relationships*.

The mother–son *relationship* reaches to the very depth of the Father's heart. How does a son give his mother to the covering/protection of another man? How does the heavenly Father watch that transferring of *relationship*?

When I stop and reflect, I ask: How does a son give his mother to the care of another man, and how does a mother give her son to be sacrificed? Mary may have sensed in her heart all the years of her Son's life He would give Himself away, but in a mother's heart, how do you watch Him die? How do you leave the place of the cross and then come under the protection of another who is not your son?

Is this the ultimate act of love, watching the sacrifice of your son, the giving away of your mother, and the taking on of a love *relationship* with someone who is not your own?

Isaiah reflects Mary's *relationship* in Isaiah 49:15, "Can a mother forget the baby at her breast and have no compassion on the child she has borne? Though she may forget, I will not forget you!"

"What is meant and represented here is the divine love and mercy in its power to transform death into life."[3] This must have been a moment of complete trust and surrender for all three of these people: Mary, Jesus, and John.

The Holocaust Survivor's Perspective

To interpret the Holocaust survivor's perspective, I sculpted him bearing a heavy cloth over his shoulders. Within the folds of the cloth is a figure of a woman. She is emaciated and surreal. He carries her in one arm, and the interwoven body goes over his shoulders; his hand holds the end of the cloth.

The Holocaust Relationship

The Holocaust survivor also has had a *relationship* laid on his shoulders. His *relationship* is the memory of the dead; it lays like a heavy weight. These are his blood relatives. For the rest of his life, he will carry the memory of them wherever he goes. He has survived the Holocaust where his own family and loved ones have perished. He was unable to save the members of his own family. If he could have, he would have carried his own mother to safety, but she too was snatched away with no one to help. The survivor now carries that burden of guilt, helpless to save his own mother.

The Holocaust survivor now finds himself in a completely unnatural *relationship* . The majority of the relatives he knew before the war have been taken, and he now carries the six million in their place.

This creates his unnatural *relationship*, now perhaps closer than all the *relationships* he knew before.

For the survivor, just like John at the crucifixion, he now carries a *relationship* that before the Holocaust he didn't have. The two unnatural *relationships* are both represented in this piece. The new but unnatural *relationship* is of Jesus giving Mary to be carried by and cared for by John, and the survivor is now carrying the new and unnatural *relationship* of the six million.

The end of the cloth is in his hand where he is primarily focused . For most of the survivors, liberation from the camps was like being born again out of a place of death. They were becoming human beings again with feelings, emotions, desires, and a fear of previous memories. Everything was taken from them; a lot of them couldn't even remember their own names.

The journey to come back to a position of reconnecting with human emotions and memory was long and difficult. This is represented in the small end of cloth in the survivor's hand. As he begins to realize what has happened to him, the cloth grows and moves up his arm. When he begins to understand the devastation to his own family, his village and country he had belonged to, the cloth starts to take on a form that goes over his shoulders then begins to fall toward the ground. The body is a part of the folds, but at this place there are six quite pronounced folds, representing the number six million murdered. These are now his new *relationships* he will bear for the rest of his life.

Summary

If God can create a *relationship* out of such a broken state of suffering, why would He replace that *relationship*? Creating "new" seems to always be a part of the character of God, to create unnatural *relationships* from the natural.

Jesus in His suffering is creating a *relationship*, a *relationship* that did not exist before the Crucifixion—not only a friend or an acquaintance but a *son* to a mother. Nothing could be deeper. Jesus in these words shows a huge importance to *relationship*, a personal commitment to it. So this then poses a question: If *relationship* and commitment are so important to Him, would He so easily replace or lessen His *relationship* with Israel? He wouldn't. The Father is committed to His people. Why would He replace the *relationship* closest to His heart?

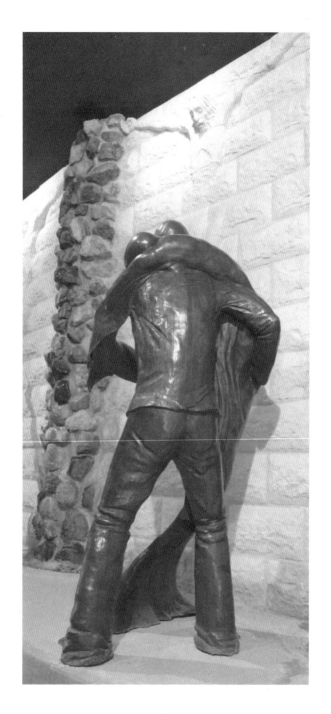

Discussion Questions

1. What verbs would you use to define the key concept *"relationship"*?
2. How would you describe the new unnatural *relationship* with John the beloved and Jesus' mother Mary?
3. How does John now practically demonstrate the second commandment, "Love your neighbor as yourself," as he takes Mary as his own mother?
4. Take a few meditation minutes and view Panel #3. Let yourself physically feel the weight of the survivor's carrying the victims murdered in the Holocaust. How does the survivor reenter life carrying this unnatural *relationship*?
5. What is your view of the parallels of new *relationship* created by Jesus giving Mary to John's care and the Holocaust survivor's new *relationship* of carrying his dead countrymen?
6. Please read the "Summary" paragraph again. Then, answer the question posed: "If *relationship* and commitment are so important to the Father, would He so easily replace or lessen His *relationship* with Israel?" (Eph. 2:16). Have the Gentiles been asked to carry the Jewish people? Look at Isaiah 49:22.
7. How does the question of the Father's *relational* commitment to Israel impact your life? How does His *relationship* fulfill Isaiah 49:15?

"My God my God, why have you forsaken me?"

Panel 4
Fourth word of the seven last words of Christ

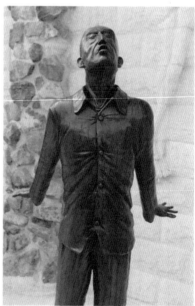

> *And at three in the afternoon Jesus cried out in a loud voice, "Eloi, Eloi, lama sabachthani?" (which means "My God, my God, why have you forsaken me?").*
> *Mark 15:34*

Key word: *Abandonment*

Objectives

In this section you will learn:

1. To establish the concept of *abandonment* from the view of the Father during the Crucifixion and the Holocaust.
2. To examine the concept and questions of the Father's perceived *abandonment* in the past and the present.
3. To explore the practical and prophetic warnings before the Holocaust to the European Jews.
4. To analyze why the author sees the Holocaust as a form of judgment.
5. To explore the relational aspects of *abandonment*, rejection, and forsakenness, as they relate to the cross and the Holocaust.

Artist's Introduction: Rick Wienecke

As I write about this fourth concept of Jesus from the cross, it brings up many more questions for me than answers. So "questions" are intentionally presented throughout this section with an emphasis on drawing attention to each question for your own reflection. These questions will be presented to you again in the discussion questions section.

Innermost Questions

Question: Could it be possible the Father would forsake the Son?

The answer must be yes, if Jesus is really asking, "Why have you forsaken me?" He is the Son described as "The only begotten Son in whom the Father is well pleased."

This question from the cross brings us to some of the central questions of life and certainly one of the innermost struggles of many Holocaust survivors:

- "How can there be a God if things like the Holocaust occur?"
- "Where was God during the Holocaust?"

Their conclusion is often "If these bad things happen, and God does not fix it or prevent it, then He must not exist."

Jesus' fourth utterance from the cross is also in the form of a question: "Why have you forsaken me?" Jesus is searching for a reason for the forsakenness. He is asking:

- "Why can I not find You or feel Your presence when I need to feel it the most?"
- "Is there a reason You have (now) left me alone?"

Identification in Abandonment

Jesus' questions are based on relationship. He knows the Father's presence. He trusts His Father and knows that if His Father is not present there must be a reason. When Jesus is in the full emotional state of the *abandonment* of God, it must touch a deep place of memory within Him. This place of questioning the Father's forsakenness allows Him to enter the full reality and identification of *abandonment*, so He can become our chief Intercessor.

Abandonment

God compares abandonment in the Bible to a form of judgment: "In a surge of anger I hid my face from you for a moment" (Isa. 54:8). In a way, He even removes Himself from the situation and cannot be found. God's presence removed from the world even for a moment could end up being years of a World War. I think this may be the greatest form of judgment.

As an example of the Father turning His face, we can look at the story of Moses. Moses takes a place of intercession between God and the Israelites' sin. God says He won't destroy them, but He will no longer be present with them. Moses then goes into great prayer and pleading with God not to remove His presence. Moses understands that there would be no life outside God's presence.

God's Momentary Abandonment

When God's face is turned toward you, He can also be correcting you, but I don't think it is as severe. His correction is determined for you to return to Him if you are in sin. His greatest show of that determination is the Father *abandoning* for a moment His most beloved Son, in order to create a way forever for salvation. The key word here is for a "moment." It is something God cannot stand. His own grace is too strong, and it pulls Him back to the cries of His people and His own Son on the cross.

Abandonment can come from God, and He will have a reason for it. We often don't have the ability to understand the answer, and most of the time we don't want an answer; we just want it to end and now! This must be a part of Jesus' identification on the cross with us. As with the Holocaust survivors, they both must have begged for the *abandonment* of their circumstances to end.

- Is it any different for us today?
- Do we beg for our perceived *abandonment* to end?

God can only live in *abandonment* from us for a moment. These *abandoned* moments might have been expressed in six years of a World War. Man is able to live in a chosen place of *abandonment* from God his whole life.

In many ways, men are not asking a question about *abandonment*; they are simply accusing God. If their accusation is genuine communication toward God and not only a self-justification, God has the right to accuse back, to communicate back. He turns His back from them for a moment, but man shows in his history he has forsaken God for thousands of years.

- What is mankind's answer for God when He asks, "Why have you deserted Me?"

Judgment and Warnings

There were definite judgments within the Holocaust but not without the Father's warnings. Because of His heart, He gave constant warnings practically and prophetically throughout the 1930s but specifically to the Jews in Germany and Europe from 1932 and 1939. Here are a few examples:

1. The Nuremburg laws were put in place in Germany, restricting the movements of the Jews.
2. Some of the Rabbis advised that the madness from Germany was temporary and that Jews should not leave the country.
3. Israel, then called Palestine, was wide open for immigration in the beginning of the 1930s. A strong Zionist leader, Zeev Jabotinsky, went

to a number of Jewish communities pleading, "Can't you smell the smoke; can't you feel the earth beneath your feet burning? Get out while you can! Get to Israel!" This was quite a strong practical and prophetic warning from a Jewish leader.

4. Palestine slowly started closing in 1936, after the beginning of Arab riots. Palestine finally closed for the Jewish people in Europe in 1939 after the British *White Paper* of the same year almost brought Jewish immigration to an end.
5. The Jews who heeded the warnings and immigrated to Palestine were saved from destruction.

The warnings, signs, and even the reports of the coming destruction were disregarded to the point Polish Jews considered their country the Promised Land and a number of their cities as Jerusalem. They embraced a replacement theology that needed to be destroyed.

I think judgment also has a defined time, a mark in the sand the Lord puts there. As judgment comes, He then looks for intercessors and prophets to help lessen the effects of what He knows man will do to his fellowman when His grace is removed momentarily.

The world lives within His grace. If His grace is removed and His face is turned away even for a moment, men behave according to their nature. They kill one another, seeking their own control. They create movements of power to belong to. This completely describes man's preparations for World War II. The fruit of that war was fifty-five million people dead in six years.

Out of the death, judgment, and the Holocaust of World War II, Israel the land was born.

- ♦ Could Israel have happened without the Holocaust?

Separation and Abandonment

- Is there a reason Jesus had to feel and know the loss of God's presence?

With Jesus this question hangs in the air, not as an accusation but as a genuine expression of the fullness of His pain. In faith He knows an answer exists for His loss, but the Father has not shown Him. Jesus must have thought during His time on the cross:

- Are there times separation from the Father is good?
- Is this forsakenness proven to be necessary?

It seems *abandonment* and loss brings some of life's most difficult questions:

- What if something terrible is happening and God is there and decides not to intervene, not to stop it, and He just lets it occur?
- Does that mean He is not there?

There were at least thirteen assassination attempts against Adolph Hitler, and all failed. Auschwitz could have been bombed long before the end of the war, but it wasn't.

- Again, where was God?

Yes, Satan has power, but God has the ultimate decision. If God is all-powerful and all knowing, He knows man's nature. He allowed man to express the full nature of his evil in the Holocaust of six million Jews.

- Does God have to turn His back in order for evil to happen?
- Is it the deepest form of judgment when He turns His back for a moment?

In God's economy this brief moment could be six years. . . . In Hebrew the expression is *asserut panim*, the "covering or removing of face, a turning away."

Summary

It must have been the most painful part for the Father to have felt the forsakenness of His Son, but for some spiritual law or principle to be fulfilled, He had to forsake His most beloved Son. He allowed His Son to know forsakenness in all its depth in order to give a lost world a possibility of redemption.

Crucifixion is in itself an act of intercession and an act of redemption. Jesus had to bring redemption into the place of forsakenness, but as high Priest and chief Intercessor He had to experience it in its fullness. He allows His people to feel *abandonment* in deep ways to understand His own sense of *abandonment*.

If they could understand the tears He sheds as a Father when He brings judgment, it would cause them to hate *abandonment* as much as He does. To forsake, *abandon*, or replace is the ultimate destructive force in relationship. God shows His hate for these three by allowing His only Son to endure the cross in order to redeem those He loves.

Discussion Questions

The following questions were presented to you during the text by the author. Please choose at least three and discuss them as a group or reflect, meditate, and/or write on them individually.

1. Could it be possible the Father would forsake the Son?
2. Is Jesus really asking, "Why have you forsaken me?"
3. How can there be a God if things like the Holocaust occur?
4. Where was God during the Holocaust?
5. Why is Jesus asking, "Why can I not find You or feel Your presence when I need to feel it the most? Is there a reason You have (now) left me alone?"
6. What is mankind's answer for God when He asks, "Why have you deserted Me?"
7. Could Israel have happened without the Holocaust?
8. Is there a reason Jesus had to feel and know the loss of God's presence?
9. Are there times separation from the Father is good?
10. Does God have to turn His back in order for evil to happen?

"I am thirsty."

Panel 5
Fifth word of the seven last words of Christ

Later, knowing that all was now completed, and so that the Scripture would be fulfilled, Jesus said, "I am thirsty."

John 19:28

Key word: *Thirst*

Objectives

In this section you will learn:

1. To identify the concept of *thirst* from different perspectives.
2. To examine the concept of *thirst* from the view of identification.
3. To analyze why Jesus experienced such extreme *thirst*.
4. To explore the principle of intercessory identification in this fifth word from Jesus.
5. To defend the principle of what extreme lengths Jesus went to identify with His own people.

Jesus As Living Water

This is the cry of Jesus; it is a personal cry, one that belongs to His own sufferings. It expresses as an inner cry, not only an immediate need. He has declared Himself to be the Giver of living water, and if any man drinks from Him he will never be *thirsty* again. If Jesus has declared Himself to be the Source of living water and He is saying He now *thirsts*, it must mean He has nothing left; He has given every drop of Himself.

Jesus' Thirst

This is why there is a sense in my Crucifixion sculpture that everything is moving downward. The fingers in the hands are surreally pulling down, the head is tilted to the side, and his mouth is hanging open. All has been drained from Him. When water is poured out, it tries to find the lowest place possible before it stops. He is our drink offering poured out to its final drop. The final drop, the last tear is shown in His feet coming to a point almost like a single droplet.

The Holocaust Figure

The figure representing the Holocaust has one hand almost touching the crucified feet, representing that last tear. The concentration camp inmates would say they had no more tears to shed. When no more emotions remain, it brings dryness to the soul.

The Holocaust Identification with Thirst

The Holocaust figure is crouched, also a downward motion—not a place of worship but an identification with being poured out. *Thirst*, from the perspective of the Holocaust, had huge identification. They said that within the camps you could survive for a long time on small pieces of bread, but if you didn't have water to drink you would be dead within a day .

The other hand of the figure representing the Holocaust is at ground level, cupped and searching for that inner water poured out. As with all men, it represents that there is a place of inner *thirst*, the unseen dryness that can kill the soul, not just the body.

A specific reflection on Auschwitz is when the prisoners arrived; they were compressed into cattle cars for days on end without food or water. A percentage of those who arrived to the camp had already died within the cars, mostly from *thirst*. Those who endured this torture could understand in the deepest way a *thirst* attached to suffering and death.

Summary

If Jesus is a spring with no end, then why is He brought to the last drop? It must be the same principle of intercessory identification as in the last word. For the Crucifixion to bring redemption to the place of *thirst*, Jesus has to know it personally.

He carried this experience fully within His own body and soul. For Him to be able to fully intercede for us, He must have full identification with *thirst*. Again, we must come to a conclusion that if He is so willing to identify with us, how much more does He identify with His own people!

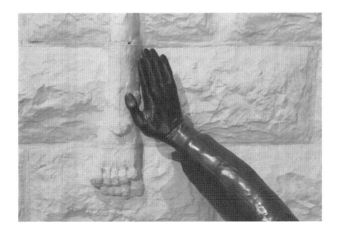

Discussion Questions

1. Jesus declared Himself to be living water. Now He is saying He *thirsts*. Discuss and explore the paradox of Jesus as providing living water and being *thirsty*.
2. The Holocaust sculpture has one hand almost touching the crucified feet of Jesus, representing that last tear. Why does the artist have the Holocaust sculpture not touch Jesus' feet?
3. What brings "the dryness of the soul"? Discuss the extreme circumstances and conditions that must have brought that dryness to the concentration camp prisoners.
4. Explore John 19:28–29 again. Why does "I am *thirsty*" fulfill the Scripture?
5. What is the principle of intercessory identification in this word?
6. The artist concludes with this question: Again, we must come to a conclusion that if He is so willing to identify with us, how much more does He identify with His own people? What is your conclusion to this question? Explore and discuss your answers.

"It is finished."

Panel 6

Sixth word of the seven last words of Christ

> When He had received the drink, Jesus said, "It is finished." With that, He bowed His head and gave up His spirit.
> John 19:30

Key word: *Finished*

Objectives

In this section you will learn:

1. To identify the concept of being *finished* from different perspectives.
2. To examine the concept of *finishing* from the view of identification.
3. To analyze what the concept of *finishing* meant to the Jews after World War II.
4. To analyze what the concept of *finishing* meant to Jesus.

A Finish to His Suffering

This is a word with significance on so many levels that you might ask, "What does it mean?" Jesus is bringing an end to His suffering. That in itself is amazing. Historically, Crucifixion could last for days. If we understand correctly, Jesus' Crucifixion was hours, not days, in length.

I have several questions about why Jesus may have died in only hours:

- Was the flogging Pilate gave Jesus before the Crucifixion so severe it shortened the length of His Crucifixion?
- If Jesus is seen as the Lamb slain for Passover, was He meant to die before Passover started?

The ruling Jews wanted the legs of those being crucified to be broken, so death would come immediately and they wouldn't be left hanging on their crosses over Passover. In the Jews religious thinking, Passover would be disturbed or somehow affected by those crucified bodies hanging during the holiday. Breaking the legs brought immediate death through suffocation. When they came to Jesus to break His legs, they were surprised, even astounded, that He was already dead. Obviously in all their experience with crucifixion they had not seen death come so quickly to the victim.

Identification to the Holocaust

Death by suffocation on the cross always got my attention in its identification with the Holocaust. Crucifixion was created to inflict the maximum amount of pain to the victim for the longest amount of time possible. The final stage of death came through suffocation when the victim couldn't push himself up to breathe. By identification, the Holocaust victims in the camps were worked and starved into a slow but sure death. In the majority of cases, death's final blow was suffocation in the gas chambers.

The Holocaust Survivor's Finish

For the Jewish people in Europe, 1945 was "The *Finish*". *Finishing* for the survivor meant that nothing was clear to them. The war was over, but what are they to do now? Those who survived the camps tried to go back to the places that would help them know who they were: their villages and homes. These were the deepest places of memory and identity for them. Their most profound memories, the ones that kept them alive in the death camps, became yet another unfathomable place of sorrow. It was as if they had vanished.

The Polish Finish

For the Polish Jews specifically, their ancestry in Poland reached back nearly 900 years. The majority of European Jews had lived in Poland. It was their greatest resource of memory as a people group. What they discovered when returning to their homes was a further devastation of their memories and history. It was as if they had not existed. Other peoples, many being the local Poles, were living in their towns and now occupied their family homes.

It is recorded history that they were not received with any warmth or sympathy on their return but with anger and rage: "How dare you come back!" As 1945 ended there was a series of pogroms and riots against the Jews throughout Poland and the Ukraine. Twenty-five thousand Jews who survived the Holocaust were killed in front of their own homes at the hands of their gentile neighbors. All was *finished*. All had vanished. All they knew was gone.

The Holocaust Sculpture

My sculpting response to the survivor's "*finish*" was to cover his face with his hand. He has lost his identity and cannot fully see. The other hand of the survivor is in the air wanting to point in a particular direction but there is none, and the hand just floats. There is nowhere to go. No one wanted the Jews in 1939, and now in 1945 after the war there was still no place for them. The only place in the world that wanted them was pre-Israel Palestine, and the British were doing everything possible to block that.

So where could they go? They had to go to the only place they knew, back to the camps. The same concentration camps they had been liberated from were now being used as refugee camps. For the survivor, this *finish* was like going back to the grave, the place that had killed and buried everything and everyone he had known. The *finish* for the survivor was a return to a former death, to a grave

Sculpting "The Finish" for Jesus

As I represented "The *Finish*" in the Crucifixion, I asked these questions:

- Was Jesus bringing death itself to an end?
- Was this now the *finish* of His intercession?
- Had He *finished* all the Father gave Him to do?

In my exploration of these questions, I sculpted the expression on His face to be strong and determined. The fingers in His hands are covering the heads of the nails. You cannot see the nails. He is making them now intentionally vanish.

Summary

For Holocaust survivors, life as they knew it vanished. The end was terrible but complete. Their false Israel and Jerusalem in Poland had to be completely destroyed in order for the real ones to be resurrected. When the war ended it was three years until the resurrection of the nation and the birth of their new land of Israel.

For something new to begin there has to be a declared completion of the old. Jesus gave Himself to this death as an act of obedience to the Father so He has full authority to bring it to an end. As He states in Revelation 21:6, "And he also said, 'It is *finished*! I am the Alpha and the Omega—the Beginning and the End'" (NLT, emphasis mine).

Discussion Questions

1. Re-read the first two paragraphs titled: "A *Finish* to His Suffering." What is your conclusion as to why Jesus died in hours and not days?
2. Reflect on the picture of Panel #6. Why do *you* think the Holocaust survivor has his hand over his face?
3. What do you say to the Holocaust survivor who has had to return to the refugee camp where he/she was incarcerated?
4. Reflect again on the picture of Panel #6, then discuss the following questions presented by the artist:
    - Was Jesus bringing death itself to an end?
    - Was this now the *finish* of His intercession?
    - Had He *finished* all the Father gave Him to do?
5. Explore and discuss the artist's summary: "Jesus had full authority to bring it to an end."

"Into your hands I commit my spirit."

Panel 7

Seventh word of the seven last words of Christ

> *Jesus called out with a loud voice, "Father, Into your hands I commit my spirit." When he had said this, he breathed his last.*
>
> Luke 23:46

Key word: *Commit*

Objectives

In this section you will learn:

1. To identify the concept of *committing* from Jesus' perspective.
2. To examine the idea of burial and resurrection from the perspectives of the cross and the Holocaust.
3. To explore the concept of what *"committing* your spirit and memory," meant to the Holocaust survivor.
4. To explore the idea of "Why the focus on the Jews?"
5. To support the author's concept of "Why the Father never forgets the Jews."

Jesus Commits His Spirit

These are the final words, the last utterance, as Jesus *commits* His spirit into the hands of the Father (the same hands that at Gethsemane pressed the cup of suffering into Jesus' hands). The Father's hands are the *only* hands that could receive Jesus' spirit.

This is also the very same God to whom Jesus cried out the question earlier "My God, my God, why have you forsaken me?" Now, He *commits* His spirit back into the hands of the Father. Jesus knows God is there as He finishes His intercession. He knew that in the Father's hands rested the hope of resurrection. It was the resurrection that proved their relationship and answered the questions.

The Crucifixion Figure

Death now settles on the body of Jesus. The crucifixion is at its lowest position possible, with nothing more to give, as all has been taken from Him. The body looks like skin pulled tight over bones. He is emptied. In His resurrection, He will be refilled to once again be the spring of living water.

In the resurrection of Jesus, we see yet another comparison between the Holocaust and Crucifixion: Jesus was buried for three days. The Jewish people were buried for three years, from 1945 to 1948. Finally, in 1948 the new State of Israel became the one place on the planet that wanted the Jewish survivors.

The Holocaust Figure

The sculpture of the Holocaust represents that "burial" between 1945 and 1948. Both parts of the Holocaust are presented here.

First, the survivor has collapsed with the heavy mantle on him that symbolizes the perished. The figure has collapsed, a mantle of death has come over him, covering him, pulling him down. The survivors had to return to the concentration camps. There was no place else for them to go. They were homeless, country-less, and broken.

It was as if the survivors and the perished were being buried together. The camps held the graves where the survivors buried all they had known. Now, between the years of 1945 and 1948, they had to climb back into the graves with the perished. I have known survivors who had to be interned in the same concentration camps for all those years between 1945 and 1948. The Holocaust's facial expression is a reaction to this interned second death. He is asking, "How long, oh Lord, is my burial?"

Secondly, a very surreal emancipated figure is interwoven into the heavy cloth, which represents the perished. The figure in the cloth is bending over and covering the survivor, his hands turned upward. It is the prayer of the perished to the survivor, "Into your hands we *commit* our spirits and our memory."

It is characteristic of survivors to constantly feel compelled to remember the dead. The memory of the perished is placed into the hands of the survivors. This is why I believe there are so many memorials for the victims of the Holocaust. These places of memory are birthed out of the same compulsion: "Into your hands we *commit* our spirit and our memory."

Why the Focus on the Jews?

People often say to me, "Why the big focus on the Jews? There were others killed in the Holocaust." True, there have been many other genocides in the world besides the Jews. Stalin killed close to twenty million in his genocide. Others include Cambodia, Rwanda, and the Armenians at the hands of the Turks.

My response is to ask a question back: "Tell me why Hitler, when he knew the war was coming to a close, used his own trains to transport Jews to Auschwitz?" These same trains could have been used to save some of his troops in Russia, but he was driven to kill Jews instead.

Why is there still a similar drive within the Muslim world to kill Jews at all costs? They are killed because they are Jews, not because they are good Jews or bad Jews, good humans or bad humans, but simply because they are Jews.

What is it about a Jew that stirs up genocide in a Hitler but at the same time causes his sufferings to be memorialized everywhere on the planet? Most countries have Holocaust memorial days, museums, monuments, plays, movies, poems, and songs to remember this genocide.

Is it only the Jews who drive that desire to express their own memory? Probably not. . . . There is a deep drive within the Jewish people to remember, but they represent less than 1 percent of the total human population. Could it be God himself that demands this memory?

Summary

Jesus was killed as "The King of the Jews." These are the last written words over His head in three languages. It was for His kingdom and His attachment to the Jews that completed His sufferings. Jesus said, "When you drink the wine and eat the bread, symbolizing His broken body and poured out blood, do this in remembrance of Me."
His last words from the cross were "into your hands I *commit* my spirit."
Into God's hands He returns as, "The King of the Jews." God has given Jesus a place of memory within human history like no other man. This can also be said for the Jewish people.

While other ancient people groups have vanished off the planet and are only marginally remembered, the Jewish people are still here. As Jesus' kingdom is remembered, so they will be remembered. They are now back in their ancient homeland and are remembered almost every day in the world press.

God has never forgotten His covenant or His promises toward them because He is a faithful Father. They are so remembered because He doesn't forget!

Discussion Questions

1. The author states: "He knew in the Father's hands rested the hope of resurrection. It was the resurrection that proved their relationship and answered the questions." Discuss why the resurrection proves the relationship between Jesus and the Father. What questions did it answer for Jesus? What questions does it answer for you?
2. Reflect on the picture of Panel #7. What do you think is the relational dialogue between the Holocaust figure and the Crucifixion figure?
3. After having read the past six sections, what is your answer to the question, "Why the big focus on the Jews?"
4. Discuss or write a summary on what you have learned about the Father keeping His promises to the Jewish people throughout these seven sections.
5. How have your views, thoughts, or prayer life been impacted by these seven sections?

Epilogue "The Butterfly" - Healing and Life

After death and burial, could there be resurrection?
The question that always seemed to be floating in the air was whether there could be a relationship between the crucifixion and the Holocaust?
Could there be something in common with the sufferings of both?
Death was obviously a part of both, but burial?
There seemed to be a similarity in time: Jesus was buried for 3 days, the Jewish people for 3 years, from the spring of 1945 to the spring of 1948 when Israel became a nation of its own.
Was this the end of burial and the beginning of resurrection?

I had created the "Butterfly" piece during my work on the wall.
The child in the crematorium had been birthed out of a book and out of music. The book was *I Never Saw Another Butterfly*, a collection of Jewish children's poetry saved out of the Holocaust from a ghetto called Terezin. The majority of these children were killed in the gas chambers of Auschwitz-Birkenau. These short poems became their last words.
The "Butterfly" poem was written by Pavel Friedmann on June 4, 1942.

When the panels and sculptures were almost finished the question of resurrection came up. Looking at the sculpture of the "Butterfly", the hand of the child goes through the crematorium door, clutching a small piece of ground – this is resurrection of the beginning of a people to a land. The child possesses it, holds on to it, but like the butterfly, he never sees it.
Like the butterfly in the piece, the resurrection is just outside of the reach of the child; he can't even feel it, but it is his.
Olive leaves, representing olive oil, cover the ground.

In Biblical times oil was used for healing and anointing. This oil would be for Israel, rising now as a nation out of the ashes of the crematoriums; it would be for her healing and for her knowing the anointing of God upon her.

I realized that this piece, the "Butterfly", would need to follow "Into your hands I commend my Spirit". The last two pieces would represent the two parts of resurrection, the land of the nation and then the people.
There would first be a physical beginning of life and then a resurrection of relationship.

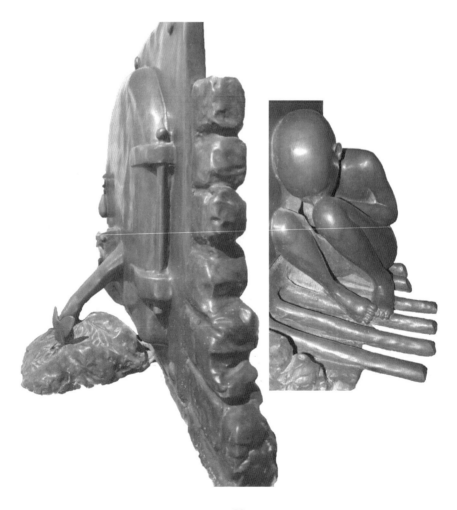

The Final Embrace and the Empty Cup

The final piece symbolizes the resurrection of relationship, the final statement of the bringing together of these two personalities. The cup of suffering in Gethsemane, then full, is now empty. Gethsemane showed that the crucifixion had been the will of the Father.

Had the cup of suffering for the Jewish people also been willed by the Father?

Half of the bodies of the two sculptures come out of the stones, stones that represented the perished.

Because Jesus willingly chose to drink the cup He now holds up the empty vessel. It gives a future hope, as they will recognize each other in a life-giving embrace.

My prayer for this curriculum is that everyone that goes through it will understand the Father's relationship to the Jewish people and to the Land. His desire is to pay back and restore all that has been taken from them. He has identified in the strongest way with their sufferings.

Within the Crucifixion and the Holocaust there is a possibility of real dialogue. My hope is that you will join in this intercession that so powerfully and intentionally belongs to Him and his tears, until the intercession is complete and Jerusalem is a praise in all the earth.

Rick Wienecke, July 2015

About the Artist: Rick Wienecke

In 1976 out of a place of desperation, Canadian Rick Wienecke began to search for God. Even though Rick was not Jewish, he felt drawn to Israel and became fascinated with the rise of this nation. He wondered how the Jewish people survived the devastation of the Holocaust -and then declaring themselves a nation in 1948 despite the constant threats of annihilation.
Rick came to the conclusion that if there was a God, He must have something to do with those Jews and this land.

A year later Rick came to Israel to work on a kibbutz for six months and ended up being there for seven years. During his years on the kibbutz, Rick's three deepest places of relationship were brought to life: his love for Jesus when he became a believer, the land and people of Israel, and his wife Dafna. Through a miracle Rick received Israeli residency, served in the IDF and fought in the First Lebanon War, and then was given full Citizenship. Rick now has been in Israel for more than thirty years.

During those early years on the kibbutz Rick's language in sculpting was born. To him, sculpting is like processing through prayer, listening to God's heart and then trying to give it a three dimensional form. Those who see the Fountain of Tears experience the intercession.

PREVIEW
of Rick Wienecke's Biography
"Seeds in the Wind"

CHAPTER 1
"This is our home! Not a museum!"

"Dad, what are you trying to do? This is crazy! This is a home, our home! Not a museum!"
Yohai, our teenage son, sounded really angry this time. He had woken up late in the afternoon after being out all night with his friends. Getting out of bed, wearing only his boxers, he had stumbled upon four elderly German ladies who were waiting in line to use our downstairs bathroom. "I am out of here!" Yohai fumed. "Dad! You're putting a sixty foot wall with seven crucifixion scenes and seven bronze figures representing the Holocaust in our backyard! Dougi* and I have been thinking about getting an apartment in Tel Aviv, and if I even see just one 'Black Hat' [ultra-Orthodox Jew] in front of our home, I'm leaving. I'm gone!" he threatened. "What were you on?"**

The day had begun normally, and during the morning hours I had been working on a commission for bronze in my studio. Even though it wasn't completed yet, we had been receiving small groups to view the sculptured exhibit in the large courtyard behind our home. The German group of about 35 people who arrived at 3 p.m. had been the reason for Yohai's outburst. My son and I were now alone in my studio, just staring at each other. Yohai's eyes were wide with rage while he waited for my response. What could I say to him? How did this all begin?

In 2005, after moving to Arad I proceeded with the assembly of the "Fountain of Tears" in our backyard. People began to talk about this project in small circles, then they began phoning to ask if they could see the art-

---

* Dougi was Yohai's friend.
** "What were you on" is a drugs related expression, meaning, "Are you stoned? Hallucinating?"

work. My family was in the process of learning how to live with a large piece of artwork that gradually was becoming public - a fact that every artist would welcome. However, all the commissioned, life-sized sculptures I had made over the years eventually had left the workshop, giving me a sense of completion.

But the "Fountain", my largest piece of art and one I struggled for a long time to make, didn't leave home but stayed in our back yard. What was more, from a Jewish viewpoint, it had been Jesus, and specifically His crucifixion, that created the Holocaust. *How could I create something that reflected the relationship between the Holocaust and the crucifixion?* I wondered. *This is crazy! Yohai is probably right. What was I thinking?*

By saying, "This is Israel!" Yohai meant something more than a geographic entity. Israel is more than a concept - it is also a nation.
Jeremiah spoke about this as well, "That I would weep day and night for the lost of my people."
My people. My **people**. Those words touched me so deeply it brought tears to my eyes. So much history has been attached to Jeremiah's tears. The ones I shed became markers, milestones along a journey that led me, the "Gentile", to be attached to this people, Israel. Could I dare to say, or perhaps whisper, "**My people**"?

So what Yohai meant was, "Don't you realize where you live? This is Israel! What you have in our backyard is very controversial." He was concerned that the ultra-Orthodox, religious Jews would stage a mass protest in front of our house.
    "I completely understand and totally agree with you," I told my son. "You have no idea how much. But Yohai, I had to create this. I just had to." The fact that I understood his frustration didn't solve the problem, but at least we had been able to speak about it.
    "If you feel you have to leave home," I told him, "you'll probably learn a lot from the experience. I want you to know that you can always come back home. But," I warned him, "I cannot undo what I have done with the 'Fountain'."

When he turned to leave the studio, I realized he was almost the same age I had been when I had left home. Even though he was younger in age, he was much more mature than I had been back then.

During their three year army service Israeli teens mature so quickly. The moment he entered the IDF (Israel Defense Force) my son would become an adult.

Alone in my studio I tried to reflect on our heated discussion.

The "Fountain" had triggered quite a few dilemmas in the past and I knew there would be more in the future. Would one of them cause him to pack up his belongings and move out? Tears stung my eyes. Was all this worth it? For what? Did I really understand what I was doing with this work, the "Fountain of Tears"? What is this stirring inside of me? Am I artistically inspired? What does it actually mean: reflection in suffering, a fellowship?

Throughout history, haven't these two personalities of the Holocaust and the Crucifixion of Jesus not always opposed each other?

My people, I thought again. *Why do I feel so attached to them? And this land, Israel, where so many have told me, "No! You don't belong here!"*

My thoughts drifted back to how it had all started, to the time I left my parent's home in Ontario, Canada. At the age of nineteen, I was on my way to Vancouver in search of new relationships and untold adventures.

TO BE CONTINUED ....

**For information on how to buy
or order this book,
please write to:**

castingseeds@gmail.com